To Ryan

Omowale

God Bless

Omowale

A compilation of poems, food for thought, and a short story

Quintin L. Noble

2nd Edition

ISBN: 978-0-615-54339-0

This book was printed in the U nited S tates of America.

• • • • ••• • ••• • ••• • •• ••••• • ••• ••

Q.N.A. 2029 Media
P.O. BOX 1067
Hiram, GA 30141
www.qna2029media.com

CONTENTS

Introduction...9

SECTION I

God Is Real 13
Visions 14
Mother, The Foundation 15
Love-Self 16
The Hand Dealt..17
Dancing Upon Nothing 18
In Love With A Fool 19
The View 20
Jealousy 21
I Can't Imagine...22
The Absence Of You 23
A Pearl In The Making 24
Learnin'...25
One On One...26
Acres Of Bondage 27
Games 28
Freedom 29
Bond Of Perfectness 30
Take A Look Around..31
Nigger 32
Fall 33
Ballin'..34
Addicted To The Cage...35
Forgotten 36
Music 37
One More Chance..38
Love Is, Love Is Not 39
Confused...40
Waiting 41
Mothers Alone 42
Two-Faced...43

My Boo And My Baby 44
Life..45
Effects Of Love..46
Strangers Amongst Strangers 47
Fathers' Neglect...48
Listen Young People 49
Super-Slab...50
Slow Killer 51
Been There, Done That...52
Jody...53
A Shameful Death 54
Gossip 55
The Darkest Hour 56
Family 57
Pounds 58
Sisters, Give Us A Chance 59
Stereotypes 60
The Letdown..61
Sorrows 62
Priceless...63
Ode To The Nubian Queens 64
Close To You 65
Stand...66
Temporary Fun 67
Shaft..68
Sidetracked..69
Dying Breed 70
You, As My Wife 71
Morals Gone 72

SECTION II

Food For Thought...75

SECTION III

A Man-Made Hell...81
Special Dedication..83
Acknowledgments 85

Dedication

This book is dedicated to 4 generations of Nubian Queens:

Mrs. Mammie Brown, Great-Grandmother
Mrs. Hettie McDonald, Grandmother
Mrs. Mildred Y. Noble, Mother
Ms. Aniyah Imani Noble, Daughter
Ms. Azuree' Keara Noble, Daughter
And special dedication to my late brother,
Mr. James F. Noble

Introduction

Omowale (pronounced Omo-wali') is derived from the Yoruban language. It means a child who has returned home, indicative of our modern language, the Prodigal Son. These writings are a direct reflection of situations experienced and also witnessed. It is my belief that one traveling the road of life can relate to at least one of these poems. In retrospect, I'm not attempting to produce an outcome, but merely to create an insight to the many problems that we as people will face. Though we can overcome our obstacles by relying on our strengths. I myself am an example of the words that I write, straying away from the positive teachings I received in my youth. Nevertheless, my being able to maintain a positive outlook albeit often times an impossible feat. It is my hope that you the reader will find some inspiring words in this compilation. I present to you this thought: "If your dreams can see success, open your eyes to your dreams."

Quintin L. Noble

God Is Real

God Is Real

When you're feeling down and find yourself filled with strife

That's when my Savior comes and takes control of your life

He takes away the heartache and turns it into joy

Satan only comes to us to rob, kill, and destroy

He preys on the weak and shies away from the strong

My Father is the King of Kings, with him I belong

He'll save us from the evil spirit—our souls God wants to lure

We all are his children; his love for us is pure

He sent his only Son to earth to be our spiritual guide

No need to doubt, no room for failure with Jesus on our side

If Satan has a hand on you, fall to your knees and pray

My God is real, He'll hear your cry and come to save the day

Visions

A man with no aspirations or dreams

Is deprived of a future, it seems

Tossed from one day to the next

Becoming hopeless and perplexed

No direction to give his seed

Not even a positive lead

Grave importance for this man to produce

Using not your gifts is naive abuse

As a Lion proclaimed ruler of his domain

A man's purpose is one of the same

He who regards not his available vision

Is one ignorant of his Divine mission

Mother, The Foundation

The definition of a Mother is the origin of anyone or anything

The term is highly comprised with great meaning

A foundation, from which we all are to grow

It's impossible to begin life without a Mother, you know!

Their position more renowned than a Queen of the wealthiest land

To be treated with respect because to us they are so grand

Mom has a cunning way of diffusing any calamity

Just by applying her unconditional love and revealing sensitivity

Whenever we are sick, Mom is the place of our refuge

A logical destination because her heart is so huge

If it wasn't for Mom, how could any of us get by?

So loyal to my Mother, for her, I would die

To receive such and honor, there is definitely none other

I get down on my knees and Thank God for my Mother

Love-Self

Before you can strive to share love with someone else

You must first understand the intriguing attributes of self

Take care of number one, which is you; then you'll have much more to give

So often passed by when you try to please others as you live

Not to be confused with self-righteousness or pride

These two terms and Love of Self should never coincide

Knowing the unlimited value of your own self-worth

Is important in comprehending why you were put here on this earth

Constantly putting yourself in bad situations seeking love

Can be accomplished by you and the Mighty One above

Your body is a temple given to you to honor and respect

The worst mistake under the sun is to inflict your own neglect

In this controversial world, love self from the beginning to the end

Just think about it, in all actuality, you are your best friend

The Hand Dealt

In considering life, it can be compared to a card game

Everyone wants a royal flush, which is tops in poker

Or the games of spades, both jokers, deuce, ace, and the king

But when we are dealt a hand with no cards of value

Sometimes it appears to be a hand full of nothing but jokers

We tend to become disorientated, and the question becomes why?

This is a question that has never truly been answered

We often long for things that are not within reach

Seldom appreciating the small victories won every day

Count your blessings; one of which you're at least a part of the game

For if you play the game long enough. A better hand will be dealt

Dancing Upon Nothing

There are many forms of dance for one, two, or many

To be done at a social event or expressed ritually

Dances include the fox trot, tango, ballet, cha-cha

Bus stop, two-step, hustle, tap-toe, tread, jig, and the hula

All these can be fun and healthy for the body

A chance to unleash frustrations when you're weary

On the contrary, there is a dance strictly for punishment

Where no music is played nor a dance floor in its arrangement

Unlike the others, this dancer is suspended in mid-air

Causing bystanders to look with a horrible stare

Neurotic movements helplessly fighting the constant swaying

A devastating situation when you're Dancing Upon Nothing

In Love With A Fool

A fool always despises wisdom and correction

What more would they do with your love and affection

Going out of your way to express your concern

Your efforts cast away in a furnace and there they burn

Everything that you do will never be enough

You sometimes wonder why put up with this stuff

Caught up in a trap with love as the key

Is a prisoner at its worst, not wanting to be free

Trying to love someone who doesn't have a care

Slowly taking you down; realize it and beware

Seeing potential in your loved one that they don't acknowledge

Will constantly keep your life on misery's edge

If you fall victim to the tragic love merry-go-round

Recognize, Accept it, and don't let it get you down

The View

Looking out of a very familiar window

Witnessing the changing seasons and a near river's flow

Watching the birds fly with such an amazing grace

I often long to take their place

Soaring to and fro as they please

Accomplishing this great feat with ease

My present world cannot compare

To the natural freedom that they share

Enslaved in a vault that seldom opens

Building my strength and endurance from within

Viewing this through the eyes of a mighty beast

Choosing human flesh as its daily feast

Devouring you at an unbelievable rate

I never considered this as my fate

Jealousy

One of man's most trifling emotions

A rage not perceived by the average notions

Envious of another's accomplishments in life

Is the breeding ground and birth of the contrite

Using valuable energy to harbor this hatred

Stunting your progress, need more be said?

Keeping up with the Joneses might seem right

Ignorant to your forthcoming plight

Everyone has their own specific talent

Locate it, and your purpose will become apparent

I Can't Imagine

I can't imagine the moon without the stars . . . . The dawn without the sun . . . . Raindrops with no place to fall . . . . A heart not capable of love . . . . A king without a queen to share his kingdom . . . . A world without children, for they are the future . . . . A universe with out its monumental wonders . . . . Territories with no governing laws . . . . Grace without mercy . . . . Fighting a spiritual war without the Savior . . . . A valley without a nearby mountaintop to eventually claim . . . . A house without a solid foundation . . . . A people with no leader . . . . Failure without success . . . . Existing but never experiencing true joy . . . . Time having an end . . . . A land where there's no peace . . . . A ship attempting to set sail with no massive waters to uphold her . . . . An eagle without its freedom . . . . A rainbow without its necessary colors, and mostly, never obtaining the full knowledge of one's whole being.

The Absence Of You

My days have been full of ups and downs

That turned for the worst because you're not around

If I didn't capture the remembrance of your smile

This course of love we share would be in denial

The day you entered my world, it was a cosmic evolution

Tattooed in my mind and forever avoiding interruption

When I'm in your midst, I'm captivated by your presence

Your smile, your voice, your movements are ingredients of your essence

A vow to be my Lady, I knew I had a rising star

Now I'm brokenhearted because I have to love you from afar

These words are a reflection of my feelings that are true

Baby, I'm lost because of the absence of you

A Pearl In The Making

If we understand how a pearl is formed

From a single grain of sand that enters a clam's shell

That is very harmful to the clam's flesh

It produces a substance that surrounds the sand in its self-defense

During the process, a valuable jewel is made

From this, we can claim the victory in a no-win situation

Shortcomings that confront us in our everyday life

Will bring about strengths that we never knew existed

Granted we acknowledge our inner power to overcome

A key thought that should always be considered

Everything that we are is God's gift to us

Everything that we become is our gift to God

Learnin'

Experience is very necessary for growth

To be handled with a conscious approach

Lessons might get the best of you

That's okay, there's more learnin' to do

When being taught, pay close attention

Knowledge awaits your apprehension

Once received, it can never be taken away

To remain with you till the end of your day

Great value in the ability to discern

Never too young to teach, never too old to learn

One On One

Taking care of business, just you and your companion

Is a sure way to strengthen this union

Keeping the third party at a reasonable distance

Giving this love a much-needed chance

Communicate and strive to be understanding and complacent

In true long-lasting romance, this is a main ingredient

Rare love is an endangered species in a world of hit-and-run

A blessing to experience the value of One on One

Acres Of Bondage

A land once used to harvest the crops

Another idea comes to mind when the plowings stops

The plot is to devise a system with a higher financial gain

Even at the expense of someone else's sorrows and pain

Displaced men enduring hard labor for a penny

The numbers of brothers here is alarming and plenty

Being treated as less than anything human

Some made strong, others reduced to mental ruin

The rest, totally clueless as to the part they're playing

A direct result of one's mentality when it's decaying

Generating billions of dollars in an area otherwise destitute

The influx of people coming and going, it's a chore to compute

Pitiful to use land for the sake of incarceration

Instead of its original purpose to produce vegetation

Games

Don't let anyone play games with your heart or mind

Many promises never kept is a beginning sign

Wanting to fill your head with eloquent speech

Be watchful of your feelings I do beseech

In a game, someone must win and someone must lose

With real love, both are winners, if you choose

Time out for playin' strictly business and keep it real

Showing respect for the way a person may feel

We are all responsible for things we say and do

The treatment you give will be returned to you

Freedom

You develop a renewed respect for freedom once you lose it

Dreaming constantly of past days, I must admit

Just to wander off seems so far away

Praying for the strength to make it from day to day

A second chance in life, you'll know how to react

Never to repeat this saga again, and that's a fact

Diligently seeking deliverance and forgiveness to the best of my ability

Life is best lived with freedom and tranquility

Bond Of Perfectness

A marriage that survives years and years
Being at the bedside of someone convalescing
Handkerchief in hand to wipe away the tears
    Love is the Nucleus
Giving what you can to the less fortunate
An encouraging word for those in need
With every man dealing fair and just
    Love is the Nucleus
Children who have gone astray
Taking paths that appear safe
Remaining their refuge anyway
    Love is the Nucleus
In these; perseverance long-suffering
Charity, meekness, kindness
Humbleness of mind and forbearing
    Love is the Nucleus

Take A Look Around

Take a careful look around
At the many faces concrete in a frown
What does it take for us to realize
The various deceits dressed in disguise
Toils and snares that are at hand
Accessories of a brilliant master plan
Prisoner of a world you can see and not touch
Life in this manner doesn't amount to much
O how the shackles placed on your feet
Reminiscent of yesterdays we will soon meet
If our brothers don't regress and reunite
And realize we are in the same fight
Divide and Conquer is an opportunity
To create chaos in our community
Eliminate the head of the household
A vicious cycle begins to unfold
As dismal as it all may sound
Observe and take a look around

Nigger

The most misinterpreted word in our vocabulary

Causing centuries of racial turmoil and controversy

Ignorantly associated with the color of one's skin

Attitude is where the definition should begin

Having no regard for another's privacy or property

Saying whatever comes to mind, acting uncontrollably

Is one aspect of the *Nigger* word's true meaning

Black Leaders have sought to correct its teaching

A term used constantly by our oppressor

Reminding us that to them we are the lesser

Now this word is adopted and used by young brothers

Calling each other Nigger and downgrading one another

Unfair to label this word upon the whole black race

We must attempt to put it in its proper place

Fall

No one is immune to failure in an imperfect world

Sunrise to Sunset, decisions must be thorough

Deviating from your original hard-thought plan

Putting yourself in a position difficult to understand

Look at each situation as a learning experience

Accept the lesson taught, and failure will prove its significance

As babies learn to crawl before they can walk

Your trials will identify actions from mere talk

Although many problems may appear unexpected and abrupt

The worst scenario of falling is to never get up

Ballin'

Round ball is enjoyed all over the world and will prevail
Not only for a male but also for a female
The exciting game of Basketball
Is played by the short and very tall
An atmosphere producing much adrenalin
Normally started when games first begin
Baseline to baseline in a fast pace
Letting no one easily score in your face
Showing many moves like high wire acrobats
And with the grace of smooth aristocrats
Going after the ball high above the rim
Chances of being stopped are very slim
Battling for positions as ancient gladiators
With intensity truly satisfying the spectators
The origin of the game is no longer a myth
Give discovery credit to James A. Naismith

Addicted To The Cage

Engulfed in a tailwind with failure as its destination

Ignorant to the formula that produces freedom instead of incarceration

While in this state of confusion, unaware of the cause or effect

Nevertheless, wearing the title of a society's reject

What makes a person a constant part of a never-ending system

Gaining loss of time and no evidence of hope within them

While in society, not being able to camouflage the scars

Set free only to return to a life behind bars

The root of the problem is money, better known as mean green

Causing you to end up in a place where you were last seen

Forgotten

Since the beginning of time, lack of memory
Has shown and proven to be costly
There are those who forgot the Creator's goodness
Spent many years wandering around in the wilderness
The struggle of our forefathers, in their homeland to stay
Many have forgotten the seriousness of their melee
Two people jointly responsible for your existence
Forgotten, too busy to grace them with an appearance
People who were in your corner when you were down
Life is lovely now, and the only thanks is a proud frown
Hard work involved in achieving your personal success
If forgotten can produce failure accompanied by stress
A fast-paced world moving forward with a multitude of sins
During the mass movement, who's forgotten? Our children
Continuing in a path we truly cannot afford
Our only salvation is in the palm of our Lord

Music

The combining of tones that propels sound
Able to reach the deepest chambers of your soul
Consoling and rewarding music is so profound
A strong relief when human pressures take a toll
A universal language understood by that of many
From medieval times to modern day, there is a presence
Rhythmic beating of drums by the tribe of Wodaabe
To swoon young ladies for their romantic acceptance
Trumpets sound to prepare soldiers for battle
It can be used in the morning for a much-needed perk
Even a crying baby is comforted by the sounds of a rattle
A means to unwind after a long day's work
Enjoyable to hear when traveling in a car
Added joy to see an artist perform music live
Appealing lyrics and sound converting them into a star
Inspirational music makes you want to strive
Gospel, Jazz, R&B, Rap, Reggae, Calypso
Blues, Rock, Country, Doo-Op, and Salsa
Many forms to choose from, played fast or slow
This world without music would be in total hysteria

One More Chance

There are times when you've made a real mess of things
Now left with the reality of the heartache it brings
Realizing the serious situation that has just taken place
Doesn't do a thing in stopping the course that it takes
If I had only done it all a different way
A common choice of words a person might say
Willing to do whatever and more to get it all back
Totally against your favor the cards seem to stack
Just another chance you believe will make it right
The chance hoped for may never be in sight
Though many bad situations may be part of the cause
They don't add up when it comes to what you've lost
The effect that is present, a heart torn sore
Drops of sorrow from your face to the pillow they pour
Someone said what doesn't kill you only makes you strong
Provided you have the strength to just go on
Time has the ability to heal many wounds
Actions can't predict results a folly to whomever assumes

Love Is, Love Is Not

Love is not, having to lower your integrity

Love is not, feeling used or being taken advantage of

Love is not, giving your all, with no signs of gratitude

Love is not, based on conditional issues

Love is not, to be viewed as a game to be played

Love is, having a mutual respect for one another

Love is, being concerned about someone

Love is, showing as well as saying

Love is, a weaving of the mind, body, and soul

Love is, an unlimited source of affection

LOVE IS THE GREATEST OF ALL COMMANDMENTS

PRAY FOR THE WISDOM TO RECOGNIZE THE DIFFERENCE

Confused

Maybe you say yes, when you really mean no
Or you cried when you wanted to laugh
Spent money, when the aim was to save
Frowned when a smile would've sufficed
Said I hate you when love is what you meant
Showed favoritism when equality was needed
Let go, when to hold on, was wise
Quit a bad habit only to start it again
Mistreated a real friend, and broke bread with an enemy
Ran away when you should've stayed
Rolled your eyes when it was best to wink
Turned your back when you could've helped
Cursed someone out instead of saying hello
Looked for love when a fling was desired
Started a war when peace was near
Lead someone on who really wasn't a part of the plan
Talked of Righteousness when evil is what you saw
Gave birth to a lie and the truth, you buried
Man will fail trying to make it alone
Knowledge of God is wisdom more precious than Gold

Waiting

Waiting and anticipating a very special event

Most important factor is to be patient

Each day like a month, each month like a year

Any type of delay along comes fear

Doubt sets in, bringing further confusion

Causing negative thoughts and creating an illusion

Always strive to keep a positive mind

That whatever happens, it's peace you'll find

Though waiting might sometimes cause you pain

There's strength in knowing that it's not in vain

Mothers Alone

It can be tough raising a child all by yourself

But watching them grow and prosper is greater than wealth

Planting in their minds the importance of a positive direction

In later years seeing the result of your hard work and dedication

They will always remember the warmth of Mommy's love

Pampering and taking care of them with the grace of a dove

Release the anger towards the Father because he left the scene

A real man would cherish a part of himself, which is his offspring

Keep on striving and be a Mother and a Father to your child

It only rains for a season, but the sun will appear in a while

Life is too short to worry about what is and what is not

Peace and joy is a virtue, and in life, that means a lot

The Father will one day realize the lack of love he's shown

Our Heavenly Father sees all things, and you're really not alone

Two-Faced

I know you've come across a so-called friend

Who changes from day to day like seasons by years' end

At times appearing to have your best interest at heart

Accomplishing this like a Hollywood actor playing a movie part

Their only concern is what can be gained from you

Not my idea of what a true friend would do

Speaking evil of you when you're not around

Falsely accusing your character a back-biter Hellbound

Having many faces that would've fooled even Einstein

Someone who really loves you can be hard to find

Like looking for a needle in a haystack

The odds of real friendship is that exact

But there is someone who cares about our every sorrow

Jesus Christ will remain the same Yesterday, Today, and Tomorrow

My Boo And My Baby

When you told me you were carrying my baby

I wondered me, a father, could it be? Just maybe

The thoughts of a little one we would share

I would show you in every way that I care

Counting the days until this miracle takes place

Watching the glow that has captured your face

Listening for every movement with my ear

Telling you every day that you are dear

I searched the whole world, and when I was through

Someone to carry my child, I'm happy it's you

A common bond that is growing from within

I'll soon be a father, a new generation will begin

Life

The breath that we breathe is inspiring

Between life and death, there is no comparing

Seeking to find the ultimate happiness

Prepare for the search can be endless

Believing material things will do the job

When that doesn't work, we get disgusted and sob

Hoping for satisfaction in a higher position in society

Is totally the opposite when it comes to one's deity

In today's world, contentment and righteousness is extremely odd

Many becoming self-reliant and turning their backs on God

Life consists of an abundance of good and bad choices

One common denominator there will be consequences

Wasting valuable time trying to determine our purpose

Fear God, and praise Him, and His laws are not grievous

Effects Of Love

Love can cause a natural high when it's real

Sometimes the effects being reason enough to miss a meal

Having your nose spread wide-open by the overflow of emotion

Prepared to exceed all boundaries to prove your true devotion

Uncontrolled feelings tend to make one merely naive

Violations committed before your eyes that you don't want to believe

Doing things you would normally keep from any considerations

With respect to your feelings, you minimize your expectations

How sweet it is for someone to love you in a real way

Casting out doubt, replacing it with assurance, causing you to stay

In the pursuit of love, there are many ways a person may act

But it all comes full circle when your loved one loves you back

Strangers Amongst Strangers

An outsider in the midst of strangers

Not able to adapt to the majority's desires

To them, your ideas and views appear to be foreign

Shunning you as an unwanted fourth of kin

The strangers are viewed by which they view

Their insinuations aren't accurate or true

Easy to denounce something they don't understand

If we were all alike, this would be a boring land

Believing that they have it all together

Opportunity at its worst, for personal disaster

Fathers' Neglect

Many of us have matured in life without a father who showed love

The Father of all will watch over us from His mighty throne above

Nurturing and taking care of all our needs from now to eternity

Be not in despair, God is on his way for they will desire pity

To bring forth a life never acknowledging one's presence

Is a travesty revealing the extent of their competence

Reproduction is not a function that requires the highest mentality

Being a Daddy as well as a father is the object of reality

The real plan for us as men is to take back our society

To be a role model to our children reaching this goal in all sincerity

Listen Young People

Don't take for granted the serious matters at bay
A living example of the things I'm about to say
School may appear to be a quest sometimes rough
Life in the real world, the elders would agree, is no bluff
Decisions made now will determine your destiny
Everything has a price, and nothing is free
The choices you have are right before your face
Choose one before it's too late for they will disappear without a trace
College, Trade School, Armed Forces, or the bottom line, Prison
Incarceration should constantly be stored in your mind
That's where you will end up if you don't spend wisely your time
Minutes turn into years, and they will soon be gone
Impossible to undo mistakes already done
We believe we can do wrong and always get away
A sudden shock when we are caught and now it's time to pay
Take heed these words and realize what you must do
Hard work and Dedication will bring success to you

Super-Slab

Rolling down the highway transporting goods
To big cities, as well as tiny towns in the woods
Many people counting on commodities truckers deliver
Pencils, paper, cars, clothes, even chicken liver
Shaky, windy city, peach city, motor city
Big Apple, Mile High, or B'ham the steel city
Engines runnin', stacks smokin', headin' down the road
Check in at the chicken coop to weigh your load
Talking in codes on your Cobra CB
Seeing exclusive views of America for free
Fuel, shower, wash clothes, and more at a truck stop
The smell of tasty food placed on your tabletop
Weird things take place at a Highway Rest Area
Some people like truckers, and even wanna marry ya
Great satisfaction, to deliver on time
Papers in hand, the consignee must sign
Call the dispatcher, mission is complete
Given new orders and back into the driver's seat
Runnin' the super-slab has nothing to do with luck
Raw skill is needed to handle the Big Truck

Slow Killer

Mysterious how we put our faith in a substance that will kill

The price is beyond range for an expensive and harmful thrill

A path that leads us down a road with many a dangerous curve

Surrounding loved ones affected the most, for that, we have some nerve

The euphoria we obtain and seek will only last but for a second

An aftermath that lasts much longer the time it can't be reckoned

Flirting with death in many ways, abusing drugs and alcohol

One thing for sure, it's part of the script; you will take a fall

Losing all possessions and love of self a result that is predestined

Upon arriving in this world, open your eyes and take it as a lesson

There is a way to cure it all; take it to the Lord in prayers

He'll pick you up, change your life, and show you that he cares

Been There, Done That

If you want to know the secret of monumental togetherness
Talk to a couple celebrating their 50th anniversary of marital bliss
If you're a slave to chemical substances trying to get away
Seek the counsel of someone with many years of sobriety
If you desire the insight to be an effective teacher
You must first adhere to the requirements of being a student
If your concern is the object of your destiny
Research has to take place to determine from whence you came
If you want to know what is required to live a long productive life
Listen to the elders wearing the glorious gray crown
If you're curious as to how people live in domestic or foreign lands
Journey there and get a firsthand look with your own eyes
If you want to know how to overcome a terrible fall
Talk to those who've fallen very low yet risen up again
If you want to know what it takes to be a good driver
You must be able to maintain that which is driven
If you want to know what it takes to eventually win
Ask those who've persevered and finished running the race
If you have many questions and not enough answers
Give them to the one who has all knowledge and can solve it

Jody

Most of us have escaped meeting the infamous Jody
Others confronted by a monogamous relationship's adversary
Separating you and your better half to a point of no return
Breaking you down with a terrible lesson to learn
Seems like Jody has the amazing crystal ball
Knowing exactly when and where the chips will fall
Having all the answers for every situation
Broadening the gap between you and your relation
Weakening a love otherwise thought as strong
Putting in question whether the two of you belong
Single mothers alone because the father is away
Is a specialty when it comes to Jody's prey
As far as degrees, He has a PhD in trickology
Trying to steal someone dear to you without apology
Understanding is one thing Jody lacks
He's dangerous like a viper, to be exact
You see the man here appears to be the only loser
But beware, ladies, because Jody has a sister
Never realizing the total damage he has done
Until he falls in love and his relationship is under the gun

A Shameful Death

Many speculations comes to mind
When thinking of occurrences after Death
Ignoring the most important matter
Whether you lived forward or kind
It is a fearful thing to die alone
No family or friends to bid you farewell
To say a nice thing or two in your behalf
No one to even realize that you're gone
Worst of all is to die in Jail
Where to mourn is foreign indeed
A home for many with hardened hearts
Their only purpose in life to assail
One can conclude the ultimate shame
To be born to live and die
Leaving behind no legacy or example to follow
And resting in a grave with no name

Gossip

Talebearers travel with mischief and falsehood
Don't expect them to utter anything good
Experts on everyone's business but their own
Never knowing when to leave well enough alone
Prying and coming up with part of the truth
Behavior most leave behind in their youth
Going to great lengths to slander a person's name
To take the focus off themselves, now, that's lame
Is the person at fault? No, definitely not
Truth is they only want something you've got
Talking about anyone or anything in sight
Though they talk just know that you are doing something right
They're suffering from a case of self-insecurity
Fueled by senseless hatred and unlimited envy
Another session has ended with the chatterbox crew
And behind each other's backs, they also talk too
This point observed and unanimously true
A gossip needs listeners in which to construe
Before passing a lie about someone else
Save the trouble and take a look at yourself

The Darkest Hour

The abyss of life can prove painful
A mountain of troubles with no relief near
Each awakening appearing dire and dreadful

Your heart twisted as that of milk being churned
Unable to think logically, perplexed and distraught
A meeting together of human poisons, solutions, daily yearned

The darkest hour manifests a minute before midnight
Faithful prayer for the strength to endure
Hang on deliverance will come in the morning light

DON'T LET THE HOPE DIE!
DON'T LET THE HOPE DIE!
DON'T LET THE HOPE DIE!

Family

Much of what is instilled in us from a child
Is taught by those closest to us, whether direct or indirect
How to carry yourself treating others work ethic etc . . .
Necessary elements that make up one's character profile
A boy learns from an elder male what it is to be a man
Knowing the needs of the people around you and eager to provide
Being led by the Great One, in order that you may lead
The backbone and center of strength enabling one to stand
A girl is instructed by an elder female on keeping her house
Managing and taking care of supplemental concerns
Which contributes to the overall success of a home
Striving as one always seeking to build up her spouse
Children basically repeat the things they see
Where there's love and respect, they adopt these traits
Influences of hatred and deceit produce an evil foundation
Someone else's example largely determines who they'll be
A family means much more than uniting for a Holiday Celebration
But showing love on the other 364 days of the year
True family love is never broken by financial or material matters
Family, a haven of subtle wickedness or the best source of inspiration

Pounds

Losing weight is serious if it interferes with your health
For any other reason, let it first be for self
Don't do it for someone else 'cause there's nothing to prove
A sincere and loving heart is what you don't want to lose
Many are overly concerned with shedding a pound or two
Self-consciously motivated, all you have to do is be you
A serious question that people should be thinking of
Can they handle the fact that there's more of you to love?
You sometimes reminisce of wearing a much smaller size
In the eyes of the one that made you, you're still a prize
You might be battling weight, another a drug addiction
You must remain strong in order to change your condition
Things might not go your way, and it really doesn't matter
Bouncing back is essential for pressing on into the future
First accept yourself, and others will do the same
And if they don't, at least you're not the blame
Society has been duped into taking things at face value
Paying less attention to the character of the person in view
So never lose hope and continue to strive
No matter what the situation, at least you're alive

Sisters, Give Us A Chance

Many years have evolved a fixed separation

Our thoughts have drastically taken a different direction

A misconception for us to think we can handle life on our own

History has vividly proven that we are oneness prone

Take time and recollect how this idea was first started

A seed carefully planted before our Ancestors departed

Divine unity can be beautiful once we do get it right

The enemy faultless in battle so together we must fight

Sisters, you are the epitome of an African Queen

A position that is less intent without the presence of a King

There are responsible brothers willing to take a firm stance

Sisters, set aside our differences and give us a chance

Stereotypes

Things are not always what they may appear
So take the time to make your judgments clear
A major error when one generalizes with the *all* word
Situating every subject into one category is absurd
All men are not what we are considered dogs
And every prince does not originate from that of frogs
All those who wear a suit and carry a briefcase
Are no more important than the blue-collar ace
All women who gain power do not become witches
And every operator of a fancy car isn't surrounded by riches
All inner-city youths do not evolve into thugs
And small-town USA isn't exempt from crime and drugs
All people are not racist nor proprietors of bigotry
But some true seekers of solutions concerning racial harmony
All those who are generous do not cover up a hidden agenda
And every relative not seen in years isn't so anxious to see ya
All systems are not geared to halt one's personal progress
And one's social status makes one no better than the rest
A leader doesn't always get results by ruling with the iron rod
The only time that all is all is in reference to God

The Letdown

As I look at a picture of my precious child
An overwhelming concern comes about me
Being a product of circumstances I feared to repeat
Putting myself in a position that hinders my obligation as a father
The exact scenario my child is presently unaware of
Although I was striving to be a good provider
Taking a gamble that would be the vehicle into this taboo world
The end result is photostatic to my experience
Another African-American sibling forced to accept
The absence of part of the team that created them
Never a fair exchange for those who suffer the most
Our siblings in a world surrounded by adult iniquities
A constant reminder of my failure is revealed
When I look into the eyes of the child in the picture
Naturally trusting that her parents would seek her well-being
Like infant birds, waiting in a nest to be fed by their producers
The infamous question that is bound to be asked
The little ones want to know where is their *Daddy?*

Sorrows

Your heart might be filled

With painful sorrow today

But in the mystery of time

There's an ability to take it all away

Priceless

There are some things that money

can't buy and so often go unnoticed by

the human eye they are never bought, only given

Ode To The Nubian Queens

More beautiful than a sunset off the Ivory Coast
So taken by my Sisters, to the world, I boast
There's cream, brown sugar, and cocoa chocolate
For us to love and respect the action most appropriate
Our whole being upheld by your contributions
Carefully guided by your love and spiritual intuitions
So stunning your countenance, a comment so true
Many envy and long to imitate your virtue
Fortunate to behold the grace to earth you bring
In such abundance that it makes my heart sing
Through your eyes, I can see a promising destiny
Unleashing my deepest emotions, setting my soul free
A delight to see regardless of the chosen attire
Another attribute in you I truly admire
Nubian Queen, you're in a class of your own
Absent of words, one's persona makes it known
You add spice and flavor to all humanity
Exposing in many ways the extent of your quality
Time has long past to receive your just due
I praise the Creator for blessing us with you

Close To You

I love to hold you in my arms
Being exposed to all of your charms
Your body is a temple of passion elite
That entraps me every time we meet
The glow about you has a beautiful shine
I'm the happiest man alive because you're mine
A kiss from your lips sends me to ecstasy
I am the lock, and you hold the only key
Feeling your body's heat from our loving embrace
Fragrance so beholding I desire a taste
Exploring your temple from head to toe
I can see it in your eyes, you love it slow
Enjoying every climax of the moment
Loving you more and more until your heart's content

Stand

No doubt it's difficult being a black man
Oppositions everywhere, but still, you must stand
A conspiracy to destroy you as early as the cradle
Stretching the male/female ratio something deemed fatal
If they destroy your mind, the body will follow
An overdose of inferiority, feeling tense and hollow
We must build up and govern our surroundings
A fearful thing in the past so massa responded with back-poundings
There's much time invested in this lopsided ideology
In the name of justice is the core of the irony
A subliminal message to be worth more incarcerated
And to be looked upon as a threat having money and being educated
Easy to control when you're ignorant of the truth
Parlaying every option to keep you aloof
They've tried an eternity our willpower to suppress
Our forefathers, if they could speak, would attest
Hard to kill a transgenerate spirit so powerful
Those at the helm are wicked and liable
Stand tall in spite of their efforts so defiant
No matter the struggle, it's a small thing to a Giant

Temporary Fun

Summer's lust achieved

Afterward, many seasons of regret

Was it worth it? Was it worth it?

Shaft

Mere words can stifle a man's financial gain
A member of the working-class poor although you complain
Verdict given, you are to live on fifty dollars a week
Your mountain climb cut short just inches from the peak
A massively complex system enough to push you over the edge
A consolation for allegedly going back on your paternal pledge
No matter how much money you used to make
A signature on a complaint makes it theirs to take
Although there are many who deserve this treatment
Innocent bystanders caught in the cross fire, a scenario very frequent
Emotions may get involved, giving great power to the evil
Somebody once near and dear turning cold with upheaval
In many cases, not being used for truth, only as a tool
To vent out anger and frustration and make us all a fool
We shouldn't have to go to someone else to solve our problems
Organize ourselves, refusing to fall prey to another system
What satisfaction is there in forcing acceptance of responsibility?
Escaping the real matter, the security of an innocent baby
To create a life and raise one involves an art and a craft
Unfortunately those striving for progress sometimes get the shaft

Sidetracked

Liquor stores on every corner
Each day brings a new mourner
Chemicals flowing in abundance
Shortchanged, in light of your finance
Force-fed certain images on TV
Stonewalled so that you don't see
The scandals that so commonly reek
Just surviving from week to week
Pigeon held in the form of bills
Not adequately paid for your skills
Every time you try to rise
Someone's planning your demise
Roundtable discussions provide another scheme
So that only a few can grab the American Dream

Dying Breed

Black men, why are we killing one another?
Displaying much animosity for your own brother
Hand-to-hand combat, shedding blood in the streets
Protecting territories and temporary treats
Taking big risks just to get paid
Money has no use where the deceased are laid
Funeral homes filled with young potential leaders
Snuffed out along with hopes deferred
Our Queens deciding to look to the left
The black race being dismantled, the greatest theft
We are finishing the farce that others began
To cease the growth of the striving black man
Enough negative influences inflicted upon us
We must learn to treat each other just

You, As My Wife

I want to spend the rest of my life with you
You've gently caressed my soul with the things that you do
The ideal lady when I think of whom to share my love
Our worlds met only by the guidance of God above
Waking up every morning being able to look into your eyes
Would be a blessing, and the joy is beyond disguise
I can't promise a rose garden, but as sure as I am born
I'll give my all to protect you from even a single harmful thorn
To assure your heart's joy, I'm willing to take every sacrifice
So faithful and true our feelings, I long to live each day twice
A foundation must involve trust in which a couple can build
To your deepest thoughts and concerns, I would definitely yield
Your strengths are my weaknesses, and the same in return
Many lessons taught by love that with you I want to learn
My heart is with you and, yours reside with me
The both of them together for the whole world to see
I know that we will have a sincere and loving family
Taking care of one another and conquering all negativity
My words would be confirmed as we stroll down the aisle
Crossing the threshold into a life, living as one worthwhile

Morals Gone

I remember when short pants was considered a sin
And afros was what you wore to prove you wanted in
When smoking a cigarette was considered big-time
And the drug of choice was a drink called moonshine
When cars were made of a solid material, namely steel
And many marriages were long-lived 'cause the love was real
When there was plenty to buy with just a dollar
And the coolest shirt was the one with the big collar
Now miniskirts is considered too much to wear
And many men and some women sport heads with no hair
Now marijuana has replaced the popular cigarette
And cocaine is what people will sell their souls to get
Now automobiles are high-priced running machines
And couples say at the altar things they don't really mean
Now a dollar won't even buy you a gallon of milk
And the best shirts are basically that of silk
Much respect has gone into the things of the world
Forgetting the promised city with gates made of pearl

Food For Thought

Food For Thought

It's funny how when you're a boy, supposedly stupid, you don't like girls that much, and then you become a man supposedly smarter, and you do all types of silly things, sometimes life-threatening, because you love them.

You're only as strong as what controls you.

An opinion is as common as the common cold, and it can reveal one's true character.

You don't have to carry yourself as if everyone loves you, 'cause they don't. You don't have to carry yourself as if everyone hates you, 'cause they don't. But you can carry yourself in a way that they will respect you.

There's no need to always believe what a person says. Observe what he/she does; that's what counts.

Prior to death for a Christian is similar to a person waiting for a much-needed vacation.

No matter if you are rich or poor or in-between, everyone pays the price to be a fool.

Everyone does not truly appreciate true love, nor do they know how to give it.

There is a lesson to be learned in every situation in life.

In Heaven, there isn't going to be everything for some and nothing for most as it is in this world; everyone will have all the blessings.

Ignorance and arrogance is a lethal combination that adds up to racism.

In certain situations, it is best not to ask questions if you're afraid of the truth, but then in acknowledging reality, you won't be in denial of the truth.

A common cover statement for infidelity is that what they don't know won't hurt them, but what you and God knows will.

You'll find out how near, dear, and revered you really are when you hit rock bottom; many will look down on you, but how many will extend a hand?

Before one can begin to change the world, one must first positively change one's own world.

Words have power, actions speak louder, but words and actions reign supreme.

Never trade a sure thing for a question mark.

Being mature is mastering the principle of separating the nonsense from progress.

Occasionally, something has to happen in order for something to happen.

The end of the day is a good time to reflect on whether your day was complete. Did you say all there was to be said and do all there was to be done? For if you were to cross over into the eternal life, there would be work left undone, but if you were blessed with a new day, you would be granted another opportunity to finish what you've started.

A Man-Made Hell

A Man-Made Hell

From the first day that visual contact was made, an automatic intuition of knowing that this was not the place to be comes to mind. The beginning of numerous weeks to be spent in tent houses with the likeness of a refugee camp or exact resemblance of *MASH*, the TV sequel. Never being safe or comfortable regardless of what weather Mother Nature may have bestowed upon us. Various bugs, ticks, mosquitoes, and flies with the rage of a savage homicidal maniac. Attacking and committing an act of aggravated assault on you, they should be sentenced to jail time. A small punishment for stepping out of line, take a pick: mop the grass, dry off the wet fence in the rain, or kill flies on the control centers' windows and place them into a cup.

Grown men of all types of backgrounds who would do harm to anyone for so much as a smirk on their face being made to perform these stupid acts. Ditto to the sort of occupation a stunt dummy would hold down. A rape of the psyche! As we progress to the main part identical to a hamster maze multiplied a trillion times. The treatment is much worse a total mockery of the Eighth Amendment. Those in control of this forsaken place are masters of deception and game playing. Crabs in a barrel, you take two steps to the exit they pull you back four, 'cause they want you to stay a while. The food that is served here, the average bear coming out of hibernation would refuse to indulge. "No thank you I already ate." Psychologically encouraging you to work or else. Packed in here like sardines, not exactly, there was more room in that can. A cocktail of personalities are present sociopath: schizophrenic, homicidal, anti-social, and self-righteous to name just a few. The oppressors themselves being victims of racial ignorance.

Ignorance is one of the worst human pains. The whistle that blows during count time reminds one of the end of a work day at the rock quarry where Fred Flintstone worked. Master Gilmore's whistle is calling for his servants to be counted and accounted for. So many counts, as if anyone is going anywhere without permission. Some have left with the idea of going home, only to end up back at the front gate begging to be let in. Having experienced a close encounter of the worst kind in the surrounding swamps. The only way to escape this work camp is by being very, very sick, lame, or totally out of your mind. Even then, they'll try to work with you—unlimited greed. Speaking of work, many guys who wouldn't work in society will work here, it's mandatory. "No talk back."

There is much more going on here than meets the average eye. Again, the oppressors, some being descendants of incest plus having backwoods theories—a mind-blowing combination. It has been proven that the offspring of incest are sometimes a couple cans short of a six-pack placed in authority to make important decisions, with a mentality appearing to be equivalent to the greasiest prisoner. This man-made hell would put Babylon plus Sodom and Gomorrah to shame with its dealings. Some of us know what went on in those places; I never witnessed so many young people walking around with missing teeth in my lifetime. You would think that everyone bit a piece of the same tainted candy. Real reason, some being naturally extracted others with their teeth missing as a result of a battle of some sort. Battles that were highly common in a place where tensions were as solid as the 100-foot wall that separated us from the outside world. Unable to count the many times my heart skipped a beat when I phoned home. Not wanting to hear any bad news. It's easy for someone to love you when the going's good.

When you end up in here, the truth is revealed. They either come to your aid or they fade away. "Too hot in the kitchen." If I was paid a dollar every time the word *stress* or *stressing* was mentioned by other sufferers, I would be a billionaire. This place is Stressland, the notorious theme park. Each day identical to the next. At one time being on the outside looking in, the outlook is much worse on the inside looking out. The *day* of wrath will one day find this place. The oppressors will be judged, as we all will, for the wrong that they've done, unless they make amends with the Creator.

THE END

Special Dedication

My Brother's Keeper

Your triumphs and defeats were also mine.
You've developed into a great man overtime.
Helping to care for my daughters in my absence,
Spoiling them, and they haven't been the same since.

Every time I hear a bike, I think of you.
That was your freedom after all you've been through.
Dwelling within you is a heart of pure gold,
Doing whatever to help, truth be told.

I ask God for understanding, mercy, and His grace,
And to know that you now reside in a better place.
God, please continue to strengthen our mother,
With reassurance that you will take care of our brother.

For no one knows the day or chosen hour,
That God will reveal the magnitude of His power.
I struggled in the beginning, but now I know
That God decides when it is time to go.

I'll do what I can to now live my life right,
So that I can one day join you in that marvelous light.
When you get to Heaven, it will be a joyous celebration,
And we will cross paths again and finish our conversation.

Although you've moved on to a life so much greater,
I won't say good bye, I'll just say, "See you later."

Acknowledgments

The Ministers

Rev. Frank Bishop, Rev. Harry Bishop, Rev. Ledale Bishop, Rev. Melvin Bishop, Bishop Marcelis Evins, Rev. Dwight Gill, Rev. Louis Grant, Rev. Grady James, Father Edwin Leahy, Rev. Aubrey McDonald, Bishop J. D. Means, Dr. Ralph Steed, Rev. Sandra Shaw, Rev. Leonidas Young.

The Families

Augustyn, Baltimore, Bishop, Brown, Blackwell, Burnett, Conklin, Donnell, Evins, Goosby, Gooden, Grant, Holmes, Holt, Kearney, McDonald, Minniefield, Moore, Moss, Newsome, Noble, Owens, Pie, Preston, Pruitt, Shabazz, Smith, Sutton, Taylor, Webb, Weeks, Woods, Woody and Wylie.